W9-BAV-326

John Singleton Copley

1738

John Singleton Copley

1815

NATIONAL GALLERY OF ART
SMITHSONIAN INSTITUTION
Washington

THE METROPOLITAN MUSEUM OF ART
New York

MUSEUM OF FINE ARTS
Boston

Exhibition Dates: NATIONAL GALLERY OF ART, *September 18 through October 31, 1965;* THE METROPOLITAN MUSEUM OF ART, *November 20, 1965, through January 2, 1966;* MUSEUM OF FINE ARTS, BOSTON, *January 22 through March 6, 1966.*

Library of Congress Catalogue Card Number: 65-24371. Printed in the United States of America by The Meriden Gravure Co., Meriden, Conn.; type set by Clarke & Way, Inc., New York, N. Y.; color plates printed in West Germany by Brüder Hartmann, West Berlin; designed by Carl F. Zahn, Museum of Fine Arts, Boston.

Contents

Foreword

JOHN SINGLETON COPLEY died in 1815. To honor the 150th anniversary of his death, the National Gallery of Art, The Metropolitan Museum of Art, and the Boston Museum of Fine Arts have arranged this exhibition to show his American work carried out before the Revolution and his paintings executed in England from 1776 on. Few painters in history have been required to make so violent an adjustment as Copley: to change in a few years from the probing realism of Colonial portraiture to the sophisticated idealization of the fashionable style in England. Yet he made this adjustment, as one can see, with extraordinary success.

The three museums are indebted to Professor Jules David Prown of Yale University for the text to this catalogue and for assistance in selecting the paintings in the exhibition. Professor Prown has devoted many years to a study of Copley, and his definitive biography of the artist and catalogue of his work will be published shortly.

So many requests to lend paintings are made these days that we are particularly grateful for the co-operation we have received. We wish especially to thank Her Majesty Queen Elizabeth for the loan of *The Three Princesses*, and we should like also to express our deep appreciation of the generosity of more than fifty private collectors and public institutions, which has helped to make this exhibition possible.

JOHN WALKER, *Director, National Gallery of Art*
JAMES J. RORIMER, *Director, The Metropolitan Museum of Art*
PERRY T. RATHBONE, *Director, Museum of Fine Arts, Boston*

Lenders

H. M. QUEEN ELIZABETH II

MR. AND MRS. GORDON ABBOTT

ADDISON GALLERY OF AMERICAN ART

MRS. COPLEY AMORY

ANONYMOUS LENDERS

THE ART INSTITUTE OF CHICAGO

THE ART MUSEUM, PRINCETON UNIVERSITY

MRS. HARRIET MOSELEY BODLEY

BOSTON ATHENAEUM

BOWDOIN COLLEGE MUSEUM OF ART

THE LORD BRABOURNE

THE BRITISH MUSEUM

CITY ART MUSEUM, ST. LOUIS

CITY OF BOSTON

THE CLEVELAND MUSEUM OF ART

THOMAS CORAM FOUNDATION FOR CHILDREN

MR. AND MRS. CHARLES E. COTTING

MR. AND MRS. EDWARD CUNNINGHAM

DR. CHARLES PELHAM CURTIS

THE DETROIT INSTITUTE OF ARTS

MR. AND MRS. LAWRENCE A. FLEISCHMAN

FOGG ART MUSEUM, HARVARD UNIVERSITY

MRS. ALLAN FORBES

MRS. THOMAS B. FOSTER

R. H. GARDINER FAMILY

HARVARD UNIVERSITY

HERITAGE FOUNDATION

THE HISTORICAL SOCIETY OF PENNSYLVANIA

Preface

THIS EXHIBITION affords a unique opportunity for our generation
to experience and study the work of *John Singleton Copley*, a painter
without peer in the history of American art until the rise of
Winslow Homer and Thomas Eakins after the Civil War. There
have been only two previous large Copley exhibitions, both of
which celebrated the bicentennial of Copley's birth. The Metropolitan Museum of Art held an exhibition in 1937; the Boston
Museum of Fine Arts presented a larger one the following year,
coincidental with the publication of the major study of Copley's
American pictures, *John Singleton Copley: American Portraits*
(Boston, 1938), by Barbara Neville Parker and Anne Bolling
Wheeler. Since that time more has been learned about Copley's
American career, largely as a result of the immeasurable contribution and stimulation provided by the Parker-Wheeler book. Moreover, Copley's English career has recently been extensively studied,
and the results of that investigation will be included in the forth-
coming two-volume monograph on Copley from which this essay
has been drawn. Our broadened understanding of Copley and his
contribution underlies this exhibition.

Much of the literature on Copley has emphasized his colonial work
and neglected the later English pictures. This has perhaps resulted
from a misdirected chauvinism, which finds in Copley's realistic
American portraits proof of the artistic fertility of his native land,
and scorns his English pictures with their increased technical vir-
tuosity as having been corrupted by decadent artistic influences in
Europe. Not only have American scholars tended to lose interest
in Copley as anything other than a curiosity after he became, to all
intents and purposes, an English artist, but English scholars have
not taken up the slack. They have paid little attention to either
portion of Copley's career. This is part of a general neglect of
English provincial and colonial art and artists, and of a profound
lack of interest over the past one hundred years in history painting.
Copley was, in fact, a vital and creative artist who produced splen-

did pictures on both sides of the Atlantic, and who continued to grow and change until old age and difficult times hardened his artistic arteries. Throughout his long and distinguished career he rose to many heights, and a number of his masterpieces have been brought together for this exhibition.

I would like to express particular thanks to William P. Campbell of the National Gallery of Art for his sympathetic collaboration on this project, and to Mrs. Angelica Rudenstine for editorial assistance.

J. D. P.

John Singleton Copley

JOHN SINGLETON COPLEY was born in Boston, probably on July 26, 1738,[1] the son of Richard and Mary Copley, who had recently emigrated from Ireland. Richard Copley owned a tobacco shop on Long Wharf in Boston. He died before young Copley was ten years old, and in May, 1748, the widow Copley married Peter Pelham, a Boston mezzotint engraver, portrait painter and schoolmaster. This alliance fortuitously brought young Copley into intimate contact with a creative and experienced artist, surely of paramount importance in directing him toward art as a career. Pelham died three years later, and Copley was again in a fatherless home. Within a few years he began to help support his family by means that lay immediately at hand in Peter Pelham's studio with its equipment for making mezzotints and paintings. At the age of fifteen he produced a mezzotint portrait of the *Reverend William Welsteed* (no. 1), the recently deceased minister of New Brick Church. Copley's mezzotint is more than close to the work of his stepfather; it is identical in some parts with Pelham's mezzotint of 1743 of the *Reverend Mr. William Cooper*. Young Copley simply selected an appropriate Pelham plate that was lying in the studio and altered it.[2] The most profound influence of Pelham upon Copley may have been his ideas about art, and the ideas available in whatever books on art theory he owned. From the very start of his artistic career, Copley was aware of and fascinated by the great unseen world of art that lay on the far side of the ocean. From the writing of art theoreticians he developed an exalted idea of the sublimity of the artistic productions of the great masters. Moreover, he learned that all types of painting were not equal, and that portraiture, the only kind of art for which there was demand in the colonies,

1. There is still some question surrounding both the date and place of Copley's birth. See H. W. Foote, "When was John Singleton Copley Born?" *New England Quarterly*, X (1937), 111–120.
2. Copley's use of Pelham's *Cooper* plate was discovered by John David Summers while doing research for my graduate seminar on American Colonial Art at Yale in the fall of 1963.

ranked far below the highest branch of the profession, history painting (historical, mythological or religious subjects). Copley, in his first few years of artistic activity, produced several history paintings. One of these, the recently located *The Return of Neptune* (no. 2), is based on an engraving of the subject by Ravenet after Casali.[3] Copley did not simply copy his source, but attempted to improve upon it, eliminating the shadows immediately behind the figures, introducing a real sea and skyscape, and adding color. He knew that an artist in colonial America had to earn his bread and butter by painting portraits, but in *The Return of Neptune* he was flexing his artistic wings for a flight that would ultimately carry him to the top of his chosen profession. The playful figures cavorting in the water in *The Return of Neptune* would someday become the tortured victims of *Watson and the Shark* and *The Siege of Gibraltar*.

3. Albert TenEyck Gardner, "A Copley Primitive," *Metropolitan Museum of Art Bulletin*, XX (April, 1962), 257–263.

1. Reverend William Welsteed. 1753

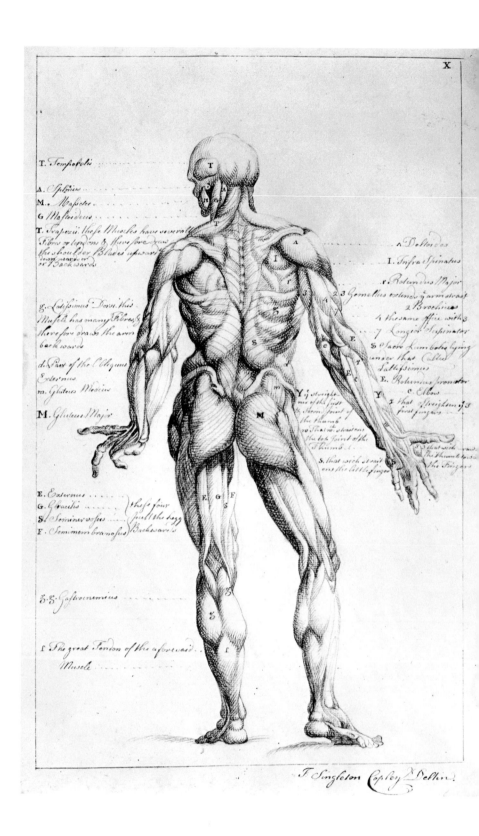

T. *Temporalis*

A. *Splenius*

M. *Masseter*

G. *Mastoideus*

T. *Trapezii these Muscles have severall Fibres or tendons & there fore draw the shoulder Blades upwards sideways or as Backwards*

g. *Latissimus Dorsi this Muscle has many Fibres & there fore draws the arm backwards*

d. *Part of the Obliquus Externus.*

m. *Gluteus Medius*

M. *Gluteus Major*

Λ *Deltoides*

I. *Infra Spinatus*

r. *Rotundus Major*

2 3 *Gemellus extends y̆ arm strait*
2 *Brachieus*
4 *the same office with 3*
7 *Longior Supinator*
S *Sacro Lumbales lying under that Called Latissimus.*

E. *Rotundus pronator*
C. *Elbow*
Y *that straightens y̆ 3 first fingers*

Y *y̆ straightens y̆ first & 2nd Joint of the thumb*
x *that straitens the 1ot Joint of the Thumb.*

S. *that with straitens the little finger*

that with the Thumb toss the Fingers

E. *Externus*
G. *Gracilis*
St. *Semines vosus*
F. *Semimembranosus*
} *these four pull the Legg Backwards*

g. g. *Gastrocnemius*

ʃ *The great Tendon of the aforesaid Muscle*

The most serious and painstaking of Copley's self-educative efforts was his careful preparation in 1756 of a book of anatomical drawings and texts (no. 3). The book digested and compressed material from two European anatomy books[4] into a compact reference work that he kept with him throughout his life. He did not go to the considerable trouble of actually learning anatomy merely to improve himself as a painter of colonial portraits. However, there was no market in Boston for history painting, in which his knowledge of anatomy could be applied; portraiture was the task at hand.

In one of his first portraits, *Mrs. Joseph Mann* (no. 4), of 1753, Copley again leaned heavily on a print source, the Isaac Beckett mezzotint after Willem Wissing of *Princess Anne*, circa 1683.[5] The broad strong highlights in the painting suggest the influence of mezzotints on his style as well as on his compositions. When he began his public career in 1753, a distinct and important period in American art had just ended. Robert Feke, the most active painter in Boston during those impressionable early years when Copley was in Pelham's studio, disappeared from view in 1750. John Smibert, like Copley's stepfather Peter Pelham, died in 1751. John Greenwood left the colonies in 1752 and never returned. Only the relatively inept Joseph Badger, and the short-lived Nathaniel Smibert, were still on the scene. In his early portraits Copley largely ignored Smibert's old-fashioned style and picked up where the younger native born artists, Feke and Greenwood, had recently left off. For example, his portrait of his stepbrother, *Charles Pelham* (no. 5), reflects the strong influence of Greenwood and Feke, with whom Copley shared a stylistic concern for linearity, planarity, clarity of parts, bold color, and strong contrasts of light and dark.

4. Bernardino Genga and Giovanni Maria Lancisi, *Anatomy Improv'd and Illustrated* (London, John Senex, 1723; first ed., Rome, 1691), and Jacob Van Der Gracht, *Anatomie der wtterlicke deelen van het Menschelick Lichaem* (The Hague, 1634, second ed., Rotterdam, 1660). See Jules David Prown, "An 'Anatomy Book' by John Singleton Copley," *Art Quarterly*, XXVI (Spring, 1963), 31–46.
5. Waldron Phoenix Belknap, *American Colonial Painting* (Cambridge, Mass., 1959), Pl. XX.

4. *Mrs. Joseph Mann.*

Charles Pelham. ca. 1754

In 1755 a skillful English painter, Joseph Blackburn, arrived in Boston, bringing with him the latest artistic fashions. Blackburn exerted a major influence on Copley, adding the final formative elements that set him on the road toward development of his own personal and highly successful style. *Ann Gardiner* (no. 6), for example, appears to have been directly influenced by one of the first paintings Blackburn did in America, the portrait of *Mrs. Margaret Sylvester Cheeseborough* of 1754 (Metropolitan Museum of Art).

The portrait of *Jane Browne* (no. 7) of 1756 shows that it did not take Copley long to learn what Blackburn had to teach him. Blackburn's rococo emphasis on color challenged and released Copley's remarkable innate capabilities as a colorist. He candidly acknowledged his debt to Blackburn in *Jane Browne* by adopting Blackburn's particular use of a painted spandrel, and placing his signature on it in a manner copied directly from Blackburn. However, Copley continued to develop a style that, surprisingly, was not polished and elegant like that of Blackburn, but strong and rugged, almost as if he deliberately chose to follow a different path. In the portrait of Jane Browne's father, *Arthur Browne* (no. 8), an Anglican minister in Portsmouth, Copley retained sharp contrasts of light and dark, reinforced by the black and white of the clerical garb, quite unlike Blackburn's softer illumination. Moreover, whereas Blackburn's colors were light and sweet, Copley continued to use strong, bright, saturated colors. The double portrait of *Mary and Elizabeth Royall* (color plate I, cat. no. 9), which might have lent itself to Blackburn's delicacy of treatment and sweetness of color, has a strong color scheme of blue and white against red drapery and is painted with remarkable power. The highlights on the drapery are vigorously brushed, and the lace is roughly indicated with squiggles of pigment applied like fingerpaint in a visually appealing shorthand. With a more subdued palette, in the impressive portrait of *Mrs. Thomas Greene* (no. 10), Copley achieved a rich and restrained harmony in the brown dress, white lace and lining, black hair and yellowish flesh tones laid on in broad strokes against the dark background. Although later works showed increased sophistication and facility of execution, he never surpassed the painterly strength of this early portrait.

COLOR PLATE I. *9. Mary and Elizabeth Royall. ca.*

Ann Gardiner. ca. 1756

7. *Jane Browne.*

Reverend Arthur Browne. 1757

10. *Mrs. Thomas Greene. ca.*

Copley enlarged his artistic vocabulary by painting oil-on-copper miniatures and pastels in a similar vigorous manner. The handsome miniature of the *Reverend Samuel Fayerweather* (no. 11), in academic garb, is an early essay (about 1758) into small-scale portraiture. The miniature is set in a simple but superb spiral gadrooned, silver frame, possibly made by Paul Revere, who is known to have supplied Copley with gold and silver miniature frames, or by Nathaniel Hurd, whose miniature Copley painted at just this time, perhaps in exchange for merchandise.

The powerful study of the Boston distiller, *Hugh Hall* (no. 12), may be Copley's first pastel. This is not an effortless performance. The picture bears the scars of his struggle to bend an obdurate medium to his will, but what the picture lacks in elegance it more than makes up in forcefulness.

11. Reverend Samuel Fayerweather. ca. 1758

12. Hugh Hall.

Copley struck a bold and beautiful color chord in the portrait of *Thaddeus Burr* (color plate II, cat. no. 13). The primary brown-blue statement of the jacket and waistcoat is echoed in the brown drapery behind the head and the dark landscape on the right beneath a blue sky and brown clouds. A splendid portrait of the Gloucester merchant *Epes Sargent* (no. 14) is obviously related in pose to *Thaddeus Burr*. Copley's portraits are often good in inverse ratio to the amount of paraphernalia with which they are cluttered, and this spare composition is particularly effective. The powerful head and the centrally placed hand, around which the composition pivots, command the viewer's attention. Copley carried his strong brush-work to a new level of accomplishment here, applying slashes of pigment freely and effectively in building up the memorable impasto-weighted hand and in modeling the head. The pensive *John Bours* (no. 15) is unusual among Copley portraits in that it is more con-cerned with the inner than with the outer man. Elegantly but simply garbed, Bours slumps in a graceful Queen Anne corner chair. Rather than confronting and dominating his environment like Epes Sargent, the more poetic Bours, a thinker not a doer, introspectively reflects upon what he has read.

By 1763, when he painted the handsome portrait of Epes Sargent's daughter, *Mrs. Nathaniel Allen* (no. 16), drawing on her gloves and gazing at the viewer with piercing dark eyes from beneath her splendid, broad-brimmed bonnet, Copley had arrived at a new phase in his stylistic development. The linearity, strong value contrasts, and intense color of the earlier portraits were now orchestrated into works of greater elegance, sophistication, and visual opulence. In three-quarter length, standing portraits like those of *Mrs. Nathaniel Allen*, *Mrs. Daniel Sargent* (no. 17), and *Mrs. Metcalf Bowler* (no. 18), Copley achieved a more convincing representation of three-dimensional forms in space than anything previously produced by an American painter. The result was hard-won, not only by the artist, but also by his patient sitters. Mrs. Daniel Sargent's son, the artist Henry Sargent, later recalled that Copley "painted a very beautiful head of my mother, who told me that she sat to him fifteen or sixteen times! six hours at a time!!!" Once, after she had sat

14. *Epes Sargent. 1759–1*

John Bours. 1758–1761

16. Mrs. Nathaniel Allen. ca. 17

Mrs. Daniel Sargent. 1763

18. *Mrs. Metcalf Bowler. ca.*

many hours, Mrs. Sargent peeked at the canvas when Copley was out of the room and "found it all rubbed out."[6]

Copley achieved similarly convincing plastic effects in other media, as in the pastel portrait of *John Scollay* (no. 19) and in the miniature portrait of his daughter, *Deborah Scollay* (no. 20), Copley's first known miniature in watercolor on ivory. A major reason for Copley's switch from a comparatively brusque to a softer and more elegant style must have been the departure of Blackburn from America in 1762. Previously most of the commissions for social portraiture had gone to Blackburn. Now, as a greater opportunity to paint stylish female portraits came Copley's way, his portraits show a revival of the stylistic influence of Blackburn.

6. William Dunlap, *History of the Rise and Progress of the Arts of Design in the United States* (New York, 1834), I, 126.

The portrait of the octogenarian *Mrs. John Powell* (no. 21), the daughter of the first great American-born silversmith, Jeremiah Dummer, is one of the first and most effective of several excellent portraits of elderly women. In 1764 Copley also painted his first large full-length portrait, the imposing *Colonel Nathaniel Sparhawk*

19. John Scollay. 1764

Mrs. John Powell. 1764

22. *Colonel Nathaniel Sparhawk.*

(no. 22). Although the juxtaposition of the rather simple colonial merchant and the grandiose setting is at first disconcerting, Copley makes the picture work by the use of a one-color costume, so that the large rose-colored area of Sparhawk himself is not dwarfed by the vastness of the architectural surroundings.

John Hancock was only twenty-seven, one year older than Copley, when he was catapulted into sudden wealth and high social position in 1764 upon the death of his uncle, Thomas Hancock, one of the

John Hancock. 1765

24. Mrs. Theodore Atkinson, Jr. 1

Henry Pelham. 1765

wealthiest and most prominent Boston merchants. Perhaps as a token of his new eminence, young Hancock commissioned Copley to paint his portrait (no. 23) the following year. In two handsome portraits of the same period, *Mrs. Theodore Atkinson* (no. 24) and *Mrs. Samuel Waldo* (color plate III, cat. no. 25), each sitter is posed at a flat tilt-top circular tea table. Mrs. Samuel Waldo has cherry-laden branches on the table before her; Mrs. Atkinson plays with a pet squirrel on a chain. Copley repeated the motif of the pet squirrel in the remarkable portrait of *Henry Pelham* (no. 26), better known as the *Boy with a Squirrel*, one of the few pictures that he painted not on commission but for personal reasons. Business was booming, and Copley found himself becoming wealthy. However, he hungered not only for prosperity but for glory. With practical success achieved, the old ambitions that had induced his early attempts at history painting began to stir once more in the back of his mind. It was fine to win plaudits in Boston, but how good was he really? How good was he if measured against the leading painters in Europe? In 1765 he painted the memorable portrait of his gifted, sixteen-year-old half-brother, Henry Pelham, and sent it to London for exhibition at the Society of Artists, where the response to it would indicate his standing. After waiting in suspense for many months, Copley learned that the picture had scored a triumph and had won extravagant praise from such leading artists as Joshua Reynolds and Benjamin West. Copley had found out what he wanted to know, and the results must have gratified him. He was good! Not only was he good by the limited standards of Boston, but his work had won acclaim in London. Of course, he was not perfect. Both Reynolds and West had pointed to his predilection for flat areas of local color, and Reynolds had also criticized coldness of color. But these minor painterly sins seemed remediable. He painted a portrait of a *Young Girl with a Bird and Dog* (*Mary Warner* [?], Toledo Museum of Art), in which he tried to correct his previous errors, and he sent it to London for the following year's exhibition. However, this time the news was disappointing. In his attempt to paint a picture that would rectify the shortcomings of the first, he produced a labored and considerably less successful one. If he wanted to rival the great painters of Europe, he would have to go there to see what Reynolds and West were talking about.

Color Plate III. *25. Mrs. Samuel Waldo. 1764*

Simple enough, perhaps, but this put Copley on the horns of a dilemma. If he followed his star to Europe, he might indeed become
the equal of the leading artists there, perhaps even a master of history painting. But what then? Would he have to remain abroad?
His Boston patrons only wanted realistic portraits, and he was already giving them that. As a practical man with a deep respect for,
and attachment to, money, Copley would not lightly abandon a
lucrative career in pursuit of a chimera. On the other hand, if he
chose to remain in Boston where he might very well continue to ac-
cumulate worldly wealth, his artistic ambitions would be stunted
and his dreams frustrated.

While Copley pondered the dilemma, he was riding the crest of his
career as a social portraitist in Boston. One of the most remarkable
characteristics of his portraits of this period is the sense of presence,
the physical entity and the personality of the sitter, that is conveyed
to us even across the span of two hundred years. The subject of the
portrait appears as a distinct, knowable, human being; as a person
rather than the representation of a person. This phenomenon is almost disconcertingly evident in the stunning immediacy of the
portrait of *Mrs. Woodbury Langdon* (no. 27), which obliterates the
void between a past long turned to dust and the quick present.

In many of his portraits Copley not only recreated the person on
canvas, but introduced realistically painted elements from the
sitter's natural environment symbolizing his role in society. In his
portrait of *Nathaniel Hurd* (no. 28), a Boston engraver and silversmith and the son of the silversmith Jacob Hurd, Copley introduced
a direct pictorial reference to Hurd's occupation. The two books on
the table before Hurd are not leatherbound mood music, but are of
specific relevance to his work. One book is identified on the spine
as "Display of Heraldry I. Guillim," a basic source of information
about coats of arms useful to Hurd in engraving family silver and
book plates. The second book has been identified by Mrs. Kathryn
Buhler as possibly Samuel Sympson's *Book of Cyphers*, a source for
monogrammed initials.[7]

7. Kathryn C. Buhler, "Three Teapots with Some Accessories," *Bulletin of the
Boston Museum of Fine Arts*, LXI, No. 324 (1963), 53.

27. *Mrs. Woodbury Langdon. 1765–*

Nathaniel Hurd. ca. 1765

29. *Nicholas Boylston.*

Hurd is dressed informally in a dressing gown with a turban on his shaved head, rather than fully accoutred in his best suit and wig. Copley subsequently used this convention for representing some of his wealthiest American sitters, as in the superb 1767 three-quarter-length portrait of the Boston merchant *Nicholas Boylston* (no. 29) of 1767. Perhaps the most memorable of Copley's portraits of elderly women is the portrait of Nicholas Boylston's mother, *Mrs. Thomas Boylston* (color plate IV, cat. no. 30), at the age of seventy. The restrained color harmony of the olive-brown satin dress and black lace shawl, against the dull yellow damask of the armchair and the very dark green-blue drapery, provides an inordinately tasteful and pleasing setting. A masterly, seated male portrait of this period is *Judge Martin Howard* (no. 31) of 1767. The scarlet judicial robes provide the kind of bold color mass Copley later used so effectively in his English pictures.

In the same year, Copley flowered as a pastellist with a number of handsome pastel portraits. The women, like *Mrs. Joseph Greene* (no. 32), were at first often posed against a background of light blue sky enlivened with white clouds. Soon, however, Copley began to use an abstract tonal background against which the figure appears in strong relief, as in *Mrs. Joseph Barrell* (no. 33). Copley found that the informal garb pioneered in *Nathaniel Hurd* and *Nicholas Boylston* was well suited to pastel portraits. One of the best of these is the quite spectacular pastel of *Jonathan Jackson* (color plate V, cat. no. 34), who is wearing a blue damask robe lined with white over a white vest, strongly contrasted against a brown background.

31. Judge Martin Howard.

Mrs. Joseph Greene. 1767

The pastel portrait of 1769 of *John Wentworth* (no. 35), Governor of New Hampshire and the highest ranking official Copley painted in the colonies, was painted almost simultaneously with Wentworth's marriage in November of that year to his cousin, *Mrs. Thedore Atkinson* (no. 24), ten days after the funeral of her first husband (and cousin also), Theodore Atkinson. Copley himself married Susanna Farnham Clarke a few days later, on November 16, 1769. Through this marriage, Copley was linked with one of the most prominent and prosperous merchant families in Boston. He had come a long way from the tobacco shop on Long Wharf, his social ascent literally accompanied by a physical one as he purchased a twenty-acre "farm" for himself and his bride near the peak of Beacon Hill, adjacent to John Hancock's house. Not only were Copley's personal fortunes now at their zenith, but he was also at a peak of his artistic powers. A cascade of superb portraits in all media flowed from his hand. His technical proficiency in pastels has been noted. At the same time he painted the beautiful watercolor-on-ivory miniature love tokens of *Samuel Cary* and *Mrs. Samuel Cary* (nos. 36 and 37). These splendid pastels, miniatures, and oil portraits like the striking portraits of *Mrs. Jerathmael Bowers* (color plate VI, cat. no. 38)[8] or the wealthy Boston merchant, *Isaac Smith* (color plate VII, cat. no. 39), and his wife (no. 40), rank among the highest achievements of Copley's American career.

8. Copley lifted the composition of this portrait from the James McArdell engraving of Reynolds's portrait of *Lady Caroline Russell*, ca. 1759.

36. *Samuel Cary. ca. 1769*   37. *Mrs. Samuel Cary. ca. 1769*

35. *Governor John Wentworth.*

Mrs. Isaac Smith. 1769

41. Jeremiah Lee.

Mrs. Jeremiah Lee. 1769

Portraits such as *Isaac Smith* make it clear that the glory of Copley's American portraiture lies in more than his ability to capture a realistic likeness for posterity or to paint fine damask drapery, clothes well cut from expensive cloth, a graceful mahogany Chippendale side chair, and such occupational symbols as a desk, writing implements and paper. It lies in all of these, plus the masterly use of composition, color, light and line to reinforce in stylistic terms the overt statement of the kind of man Isaac Smith is. The dominant area in the picture is the head. The light stockinged legs form an arrow directing attention to the head, and the light tracery of the quill pen also arches toward it like a pointer. The outline of the back and shoulders, the inner edge of the jacket against the vest, and the dramatic and insistent rhythmic line of the gold buttons, all force the viewer's eye to the sitter's head. The rich sonority of the deeply saturated colors echoes the richness of the material environment in which Isaac Smith existed. The colors are not frivolous or gay, but deep, serious, and sober. The light and dark contrasts are crisp, with the highlighted portion of the head and wig, the cuffs and hands, the paper, the quill and the stockings standing out decisively from the subdued remainder of the picture surface. In sum, the depiction of Isaac Smith as a man of material well-being, of sobriety, of strength, of decisiveness, is powerfully reinforced by the stylistic means employed.

Mrs. Isaac Smith sinks more comfortably into an upholstered armchair, holding a luscious and fully ripe bunch of grapes in her lap. The palette is in a brighter, more light-hearted key. Whereas Mr. Smith is seen as a man of affairs in a businesslike attitude, Mrs. Smith, who calmly regards the viewer, is given an air of comfortable domesticity. There is a sense of softness, lushness, abundance, fruitfulness.

The full-length portraits of *Jeremiah Lee* and *Mrs. Jeremiah Lee* (nos. 41 and 42) repeat the pictorial means and effects of the Isaac Smith portraits. *Jeremiah Lee*, a wealthy Marblehead merchant, is posed in an elaborate setting. He too is presented as a man of affairs, standing at a table holding a letter, hand on hip, in complete control of the situation. Again numerous lines, from the quill pen to the great embroidered banding on his waistcoat, converge on the head. The portrait of *Mrs. Lee* is, like that of *Mrs. Isaac Smith*, lighter in key but still coloristically rich.

In a highly successful portrait, *Mrs. Ezekiel Goldthwait* sits at a round tilt-top table, corpulent and friendly, her left hand extended over a succulent still life of apples, peaches and pears (color plate VIII, cat. no. 43). The loving delineation of the stuffs in this picture celebrates the material reality of Mrs. Goldthwait and her world. The still life is a barely disguised symbol of fecundity, and her extended hand emphasizes her identification with it. The mother of fourteen children, as well as a green-thumbed gardener whose elaborate plantings were noted in the community, her fertile touch is no secret in this portrait. The picture bulges with rounded forms; the fruit, the bowl, the oversized column in the background, the tabletop, the pearls around the sitter's neck, and the cap around her head, all echo the plump figure of Mrs. Goldthwait herself and emphasize the sense of amplitude and plenty.

In comparison with the portraits of *Mrs. Isaac Smith* and *Mrs. Jeremiah Lee*, a strengthening of the light–dark contrasts and a darkening of the palette are evident in *Mrs. Ezekiel Goldthwait*. These are the basic elements in a change that occurred in Copley's style in 1769–70. It manifested itself more strongly at first in pastels, such as *Jonathan Jackson* (no. 34), and then in half-length portraits such as *Mrs. Samuel Watts* (no. 44), whose head is dramatically lit against a very dark background.

Paul Revere (no. 45), a Boston silversmith like *Nathaniel Hurd* (no. 28), is seated in shirtsleeves behind his work table, on which are scattered engraving tools. His left hand holds a silver teapot upon a hammering pillow. Copley portrays Revere at a moment when the teapot has been completed, and the smooth surface awaits the decorative tooling. The light flows in from the left, modeling and giving texture to the chill and gleaming silver, the warmly reflective mahogany, the soft flesh and hair, the crisp shirt and the vest. No other picture shows more clearly Copley's artistic kinship with realistic Dutch masters such as Vermeer and de Hooch, who also painted for a materialistic, Protestant society.

44. Mrs. Samuel Watts. ca. 1770

COLOR PLATE VII. *39. Isaac Smith.*

Paul Revere. 1768–1770

46. *Mrs. Humphrey Devereux.*

In the spring of 1770 Copley received a letter from his old friend and early source of influence, John Greenwood, in London, ordering a "Portrait of my Hond. Mother, who resides at present nigh Marblehead, but is often in Boston. as I have of late enter'd into conections, that may probably keep me longer in London than I coud wish, I am very desirous of seeing the good Lady's Face as she now appears, with old age creeping upon her."[9] *Mrs. Humphrey Devereux* (no. 46), John Greenwood's mother, is seated like Paul Revere at a table with one hand cupped beneath her chin. The portrait is restrained in color, with maximum concentration upon the quick vitality of the sitter, her alert dark eyes flashing in her tanned face.

In 1771 Copley spent the second half of the year in New York, painting a series of strong portraits in his new severe style. His reputation had been carried from Boston to New York in a variety of ways, but with particular effectiveness by the striking portrait of *General Thomas Gage* (no. 47), commander-in-chief of the British Army in North America. Captain John Small wrote to Copley from British headquarters in New York on October 29, 1769, that "Your picture of the General is universally acknowledg'd to be a very masterly performance, elegantly finish'd, and a most striking Likeness; in short it has every property that Genius, Judgement and attention can bestow on it."[10]

Copley returned to Boston early in 1772. Young John Trumbull, a student at Harvard, visited him then at his splendid establishment on Beacon Hill and later recalled, "We found Mr. Copley dressed to receive a party of friends at dinner. I remember his dress and appearance—an elegant looking man, dressed in a fine maroon cloth, with gilt buttons—this was dazzling to my unpracticed eye!—but his paintings, the first I had ever seen deserving the name, riveted, absorbed my attention, and renewed all my desire to enter upon such a pursuit."[11] However, although Copley was on top of the

9. Guernsey Jones, ed., *Letters & Papers of John Singleton Copley and Henry Pelham*, Vol. LXXI of *The Massachusetts Historical Society Collections* (Boston, 1914), 81.
10. *Ibid.*, 77.
11. Theodore Sizer, ed., *The Autobiography of Colonel John Trumbull* (New Haven, Conn., 1953), 11.

General the Hon.ble Thos. G
OB.t 1788

47. *General Thomas Gage. 1768-*

Samuel Adams. 1770–1772

world, that world was breaking up. The American colonies were moving toward Revolution. One of Copley's best-known portraits represents a leading actor in the political drama then unfolding in Boston, *Samuel Adams* (no. 48), posed as he had appeared when he confronted Gov. Thomas Hutchinson after the Boston Massacre of March 5, 1770. No other Copley portrait is as taut with dramatic intensity as the sombre *Samuel Adams*. The dominant pictorial element, the sharply illuminated head, stands out with clarity against the dark warm background. The sharply drawn face is a mobile mask, the eyes fixed in a compelling stare, conveying a sense of the force and intensity of Adams' personality.

Copley was painting for a clientele that was splitting into two factions that opposed each other with increasing bitterness. He sought to remain neutral, and was able to paint high Tories like *Thomas Gage, John Wentworth*, and *Thomas Flucker* (no. 49), Secretary of the Province, while at the same time getting business from radicals like *Paul Revere, John Hancock*, and *Samuel Adams*. Copley felt that art and politics did not mix, and had earlier advised Benjamin West that he was "desireous of avoideing every imputation of party spir[it], Political contests being neighther pleasing to an artist or advantageous to the Art itself."[12] But fence straddling was difficult, and as soon as he chose sides he would alienate half of his potential clientele. Suddenly his early dream of a study trip to Europe seemed to offer a logical way out of a difficult situation, and he began to make plans for it.

The sobriety and strength of Copley's late American style made it particularly effective for male portraits, but he also employed it tellingly in female portraits, such as the superb *Mrs. Richard Skinner* (color plate IX, cat. no. 50) and a brilliant three–quarter-length portrait of the second *Mrs. Moses Gill* (no. 51). As in most of the late portraits, the figure of Mrs. Gill is set quite low on the canvas, and the vigorous and assured brushwork anticipates achievements in England.

12. *Copley-Pelham Letters*, 98. November 24, 1770.

Thomas Flucker. 1770–1772

71

51. *Mrs. Moses Gill. ca.*

Reverend Thomas Cary. 1773

73

The seated figure of the Newburyport Congregational minister, the *Reverend Thomas Cary* (no. 52), is another impressive three-quarter-length portrait produced in 1773. Cary is surrounded by books in his study, his raised eyebrows giving him an unministerially puckish expression. Copley appears to have posed a sitter similarly in a Windsor chair for the first time in the previous year in the portrait of the vigorous octogenarian, *Eleazer Tyng* (no. 53). Another portrait of 1773 represents *John Winthrop* (no. 54), a professor at Harvard, sitting at his telescope. The telescope makes the landscape opening to the right, infrequent in seated male portraits, a functional necessity.

Copley's double portrait, painted in 1773, of a pair of prominent visiting Philadelphians, *Mr. and Mrs. Thomas Mifflin* (no. 55), was his first multi-figure canvas since the *Royall Sisters* (no. 9), painted fifteen years earlier. Compositionally he simply juxtaposed two three-quarter-length portraits, sliding Mrs. Mifflin in a foreground plane in front of her husband, who is set in a second plane. Thomas Mifflin was a radical Whig who, two years later, was Quartermaster General of the Revolutionary Army; he was subsequently a member of the First Continental Congress and Governor of Pennsylvania. Having at this time an important client as politically radical as Thomas Mifflin characterizes Copley's predicament. Only three months later a raging Whig mob smashed the windows in the house of his father-in-law, Richard Clarke, a prominent Tory who, as principal agent for the East India Company in Boston, was a major consignee of the taxed tea which had arrived in the port of Boston from England. Clarke and his two sons took refuge on Castle William in Boston Harbor, and Copley found himself cast in the role of a mediator shuttling between his in-laws and the radical leaders. In the middle of one spring night in 1774, a mob even appeared at Copley's house, and it was only with difficulty that he persuaded them that he was not sheltering the Loyalist George Watson. He noted the next day, "what if Mr. Watson had stayed (as I pressed him to) to spend the night. I must either have given up a friend to the insult of a Mob or had my house pulled down and perhaps my family murthered."[13]

13. *Ibid.*, 218–219.

Eleazer Tyng. 1772

54. *John Winthrop. ca.*

Mr. and Mrs. Thomas Mifflin. 1773

56. *Mr. and Mrs. Isaac Winslow.*

Copley painted only a handful of pictures in troubled 1774 before departing from Boston. One of the last, and certainly the most ambitious, *Mr. and Mrs. Isaac Winslow* (no. 56), is a double portrait of Susanna Copley's uncle, Isaac Winslow, and his second wife. The composition is horizontal and the two figures are better integrated spatially than in the *Mifflin* double portrait.

Copley sailed from America on June 10, 1774, never to return. He arrived in England early in June, and after a month and a half in London set off for Rome via Paris in the company of George Carter, an English artist.

Roman Conquest. 1774–1775

The drawing known as *Roman Conquest* (no. 57) is one of the few surviving examples of Copley's Roman studies. *The Ascension* (no. 58), painted when it got too cold to study in the galleries, was probably his first painting after leaving the American colonies, and it was his first original history painting. He began it by sketching and refining the general disposition of the figures, assigning them poses, gestures and expressions appropriate to the miraculous event and planning the effects of light and shadow upon the figures. The whole composition was then redrawn in clean outline (no. 59), the light and shade washed in with bistre, and the expression and detail of heads and hands carried forward by posing himself in front of a mirror. He then squared the drawing, transferred the design to canvas, and hired a model to pose for hands, heads, and feet.

Copley was elated by his achievement with *The Ascension*. He boasted to his family in Boston that Piranesi had praised the picture and that the Scottish artist Gavin Hamilton had told him that "he never saw a finer Composition in his life, and that he knows no one who can equil it; that it is a subject the most dificult I could have ingaged in, that there is no subject but I can compose with less Dificulty."[14]

Copley took a trip to Naples in January, 1775, also visiting Pompeii and Herculaneum. In Naples he struck up a friendship with Mr. and Mrs. Ralph Izard of Charleston, S. C., and accompanied them to Paestum. Upon returning to Rome he painted a large double portrait of them (color plate X, cat. no. 60), posed amidst an assortment of classical material, including a vase in the manner of the Niobid Painter and a cast of the Orestes and Electra group, with the Colosseum in the background. As with *The Ascension*, he was pleased with the double portrait which, he felt, would "support its merrit in any Cumpany whatever."[15]

Copley left Rome for Parma early in June, 1775, to copy Correggio's *Holy Family with St. Jerome*. The first part of his stay there was clouded by deepening concern for the safety of his family as reports of events at Lexington and Concord reached him. However, he was

14. *Ibid.*, 300. March 14, 1775.
15. *Ibid.*

Color Plate IX. *50. Mrs. Richard Skinner.*

soon relieved by news that they had arrived safely in England. As for the fate of his country, Copley was convinced that, despite the turmoil and present distress, all would work out well for America. Earlier in the year he had written to Henry Pelham, "poor America! I hope the best but I fear the worst. yet certain I am She will finially Imerge from he[r] present Callamity and become a Mighty Empire. and it is a pleasing reflection that I shall stand amongst the first of the Artists that shall have led that Country to the Knowledge and cultivation of the fine Arts, happy in the pleasing reflection that they will one Day shine with a luster not inferior to what they have done in Greece or Rome in my Native Country." Now that fighting had begun, he openly predicted victory and independence for the American colonies.[16]

After completing the copy of the Correggio, he set out for Venice and then for London by way of Germany and the Low Countries. He was reunited with his family in London early in October, 1775. At the age of thirty-seven, he stood upon the threshold of a new career.

Moving with his family into a commodious house on Leicester Square, Copley undertook his first painting in England, *The Copley Family* (color plate XI, cat. no. 61), a hymn of contentment on the reunion of the family. The artist, holding plans or drawings symbolic of his art, the key to future fame and fortune, regards the viewer from his background niche surrounded by four lovely children, his beautiful and charming wife, and his prosperous and respected father-in-law, Richard Clarke. The oldest child, Elizabeth, stands in the center between two groups of three figures. John Singleton, Jr. stands by his seated mother, his left arm bending up around her neck, their eyes almost engaged. Mary is on the sofa leaning against her mother. When Copley began to paint the picture, he intended the infant on Richard Clarke's lap to be his youngest son, Clarke, left behind in America. However, the infant died early in 1776, and in the final version the baby is certainly Susanna, who was born in England in October, 1776. The compositional motif of the vase and column on the left, particularly evident in the lively oil sketch for

16. *Ibid.*, 301; Martha Babcock Amory, *The Domestic and Artistic Life of John Singleton Copley, R.A.* (Boston, 1882), 57–58, 62.

58. *The Ascension.*

tudy for The Ascension. 1774–1775

62. Sketch for The Copley Family. 1776

COLOR PLATE XI. *61. The Copley Family. 1776-*

The Copley Family (no. 62), echoes the *Izard* double portrait. *The Copley Family* was exhibited at the Royal Academy in 1777, together with *The Nativity*, a currently unlocated painting known only through engravings and a few drawings. One of these is the drapery study for the figure of the Virgin (no. 63).

The free brushwork that energizes Copley's English pictures, particularly the oil sketches, is very evident in the spirited *Self-Portrait* (no. 64). Here, more than in *The Copley Family*, the artist's likeness accords with the unfriendly description given by his erstwhile traveling companion, George Carter, that "he was very thin, pale, a little pock-marked, prominent eyebrows, small eyes, which, after fatigue, seemed a day's march in his head."[17] The splendid 1778 portrait of

17. Allan Cunningham, *The Lives of the Most Eminent British Painters and Sculptors*, IV (New York, 1834), 144.

63. Study for The Nativity. 1776

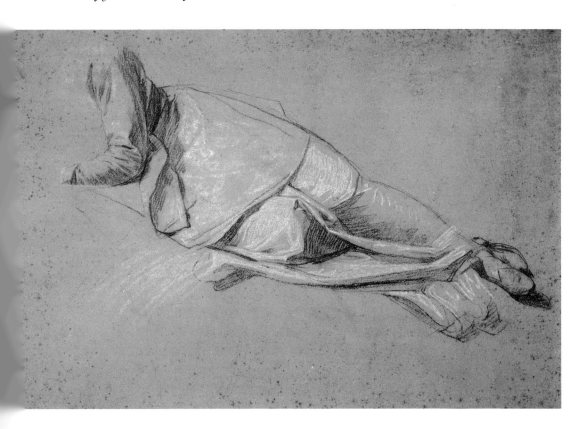

Squire Robert Hyde of Hyde (no. 65), in contrast with American portraits like *Thomas Flucker* (no. 49), also reveals the increased freedom of brushwork and the lightening of the palette in Copley's early English portraits.

Copley followed his own family picture with another one, *The Pepperrell Family* (no. 66), exhibited at the Royal Academy in 1778. A tightly drawn study for the figure of Sir William Pepperrell (no. 67), delicately squared for transfer, is, like *The Nativity* drawing, a detailed drapery study with careful attention to the effect of light.

64. Self-Portrait. 1776–

Squire Robert Hyde of Hyde. 1778

66. Sir William Pepperrell and His Family.

Study for Sir William Pepperell and His Family. 1777–1778

Although Copley concentrated on portraiture during his first few years in London in order to support his family, he did not put aside his aspirations toward the highest branch of his profession, history painting. An opportunity to depart from portraiture came in a commission from Brook Watson. In *Watson and the Shark* (color plate XII, cat. no. 68a), Copley recorded a horrible scene from Watson's youth when, in 1749 at the age of fourteen, he had been attacked by a shark while swimming in Havana harbor. The painting, also exhibited at the Academy in 1778, greatly extended Copley's reputation. It was a striking and remarkable picture, well calculated to catch the public fancy. The composition is built about the strong horizontals of the boy and the shark, the boat, the cityscape, and

68b. Watson and the Shark.

Morro Castle in the background. These horizontals are not exactly parallel on the surface, and form a zig-zag recession in space. This gentle movement serves as a foil to the violent, vertical accent of the harpoon thrust. The movement of the shark toward the boy, the progress of the boat toward the shark, and the strength of the compositional line of the harpoon invoke a powerful sense of impending impact. The question is whether the impact will be between the

Head of a Negro. 1777–1783

shark and the boy, or the harpoon and the shark. The effect is ampli-
fied by the theatrical light that flows in from the left: it highlights
the boy, the shark, and the reaching figures; it casts the bow and
stern into contrasting shadow areas; it picks up the stem with a
triangle of light that accentuates the tip of the harpoon.

The superb *Head of a Negro* (no. 69), has been known for over a
century as a sketch for *Watson and the Shark.* Indeed it may have
been so intended, even though the expression bears little resemblance
to the less animated face of the Negro who appears in that picture.

During the next two years Copley was largely occupied with a
much more ambitious history picture, *The Death of the Earl of
Chatham* (no. 70). This picture commemorated an event that had
occurred in the House of Lords on April 7, 1778. The infirm

71. Sketch for The Death of the Earl of Chatham. 1

William Pitt, Earl of Chatham, rose to speak in a debate on the war with the American colonies, but swooned, the victim of a stroke to which he shortly afterward succumbed. Copley saw in Chatham's dramatic exit an opportunity to follow up *Watson and the Shark* with a painting of an event of major historic importance. The path he intended to follow as a history painter had already been blazed by Benjamin West, whose youthful imagination, like Copley's, had been fired in colonial America with dreams of gaining fame and glory as a painter of historical subjects. West, history painter to the King since 1772, had already made his dreams a reality. With paintings such as *The Death of General Wolfe*, painted while Copley was still in Boston, West had revolutionized history painting by putting the subject in realistic modern dress rather than cloaking it in classical respectability. However, West had cushioned the shock

The Death of the Earl of Chatham. 1779–1781

of immediacy by representing a death scene that was at least far removed geographically. Copley now chose a subject that stripped away even that distance between the viewer and the event depicted. The scene was recent in time and local in place, and the realism of *The Death of Chatham*, which included actual portraits of over fifty noblemen who had been present at the event, had a jolting immediacy in a pre-camera era.

The composition was developed through numerous drawings and oil sketches during 1779. It culminated in an oil sketch (no. 71), which placed the scene in a theatrical setting marked by a drawn curtain on the right. A flood of light pours in through an opening in the end wall above the throne, illuminating a composition that is very close to the final arrangement. The handling suggests that life portraits of perhaps half of the figures had been taken and intro-

72. Study of Richard Brocklesby
for The Death of the Earl of Chatham. 1779–

Elkanah Watson. 1782

duced. Copley drew likenesses of some of the figures to be included, such as the scaled drawing of the physician, *Richard Brocklesby* (no. 72), but many portraits were undoubtedly painted directly onto the large canvas.

The Death of Chatham, completed by the spring of 1781, was a complete success. Almost twenty thousand people saw the picture during its first six weeks on exhibition. This success cemented Copley's ties with England and rendered his return to America increasingly unlikely. His dream of winning fame as a history painter had come true. However, he had by no means forgotten America or Americans. In 1782, while he was painting the vigorous portrait of an American, *Elkanah Watson* (no. 73), he accompanied Watson to hear George III make the announcement of American independence. Afterwards, according to Watson, Copley rushed back to his studio and painted an American flag on the ship in the left distance of the picture, thus raising the first American flag in England after the colonies received their independence.[18]

Although Copley had been elected to full membership in the Royal Academy in 1779 after his success with *Watson and the Shark*, *The Death of Chatham* had made it difficult for him to find time to paint the required diploma picture. However, in 1782 he finally painted *The Tribute Money* (no. 74) as his "tribute" to the Academy. Although it recalls seventeenth-century compositions, the handling is pure eighteenth century and pure Copley, with characteristic strength of light and dark contrasts and of color. The single figure of Christ with arm upraised, cloaked in brilliant red and blue and flooded by light, balances the entire group of five figures on the left.

Copley was at the peak of his English career in the early 1780's, and during the next few years he produced a number of pictures that in their bravura brushwork, brilliant lightened palette, and masterful chiaroscuro rival the more sober triumphs of his American style. Ranking high among the portraits in this group are the superb *Midshipman Augustus Brine* (color plate XIII, cat. no. 75), and *Lord*

18. Winslow C. Watson, ed., *Men and Times of the Revolution: or Memoirs of Elkanah Watson, 1777–1842* (New York, 1856), 177.

74. *The Tribute Money. 1782*

Mansfield (no. 76), the latter exhibited at the Royal Academy in
1783. Copley moved in 1783 from Leicester Square to an "elegant
& well-furnished" house on George Street, just below Hanover
Square. This remained the Copley home not only for the rest of the
artist's life but throughout the long career of his distinguished son,
John Singleton Copley, Jr., who became Baron Lyndhurst, thrice
Lord Chancellor under Queen Victoria. At the time of the move to
George Street, Copley was well advanced toward the completion
of his boldest and most successful history picture, *The Death of
Major Peirson* (no. 77).

76. William Murray, First Earl of Mansfield.

On the night of January 5–6, 1781, a French force of about nine hundred troops had landed on the Isle of Jersey. The invaders quickly seized control of the capital, St. Helier, and imprisoned the commandant of the British forces. Twenty-four-year-old Major Francis Peirson took command of the uncapitulating British troops on the island and countermarched on St. Helier. After a brisk pitched battle, Peirson's men recaptured the town and crushed the invasion, but at the moment of triumph Peirson was mortally wounded by enemy fire. His death, and the exacting of revenge by his black servant on the Frenchman who had fired the fatal shot, was the theme of Copley's painting.

In the picture Copley emphasizes the stir of arms and the color, smell, and confusion of battle. The spice of realism is added through an accurate portrayal of the locale and the inclusion of some participants. The representation is further flavored by the emotional

The Death of Major Peirson. 1782–1784

overtones of a subject which records the triumph of British arms rebounding from the brink of defeat, the poignancy of the death of a young hero cut down at the hour of his glory, the vengeance exacted by the Negro servant, and the selfless devotion of an expiring British drummer who ignores his own wound to lament his lost leader.

In addition to the portraits of actual participants, there are, according to a family tradition that is probably correct, some family portraits introduced in the group on the right (see no. 78). The figure on the far right with arms raised is Mrs. Copley; the other woman is a family nurse; the boy is John Singleton Copley, Jr.; and the babe in arms could be the infant Jonathan, born in February, 1782.

An exceptionally interesting drawing (no. 79) depicts Captain Clephane holding his sword above his head and striding over slain figures. The drawing also contains a rough approximation of the French group, squared for transfer, as it appears in the finished painting. There is a scale in feet in the lower right. Over the drawing are jotted notations on the color and style of the uniforms of the British, the French, and the Jersey militia, and a color code is given on the left to accord with marks placed on the uniforms of the French officers. This methodical effort to be as factually accurate as possible is as typical of Copley's history paintings as of his portraits in colonial Boston.

The Death of Major Peirson was exhibited on May 22, 1784, and once more the public turned out in great numbers. Royal approbation of the picture brought Copley an opportunity to paint portraits of the royal princesses Sophia, Mary, and Amelia in a conversation piece. One of the most exuberant of all Copley paintings, *The Daughters of George III* (color plate XIV, cat. no. 80) is as fresh as an oil sketch despite the fact that Copley took extraordinary pains with the picture, exasperating the young princesses with his demands upon their time. The freely brushed, light colors float on the surface. This was an important picture for Copley, since success with it could vault him into the ranks of fashionable portraitists. He sent the picture to the annual exhibition at the Royal Academy in the spring of 1785.

Unfortunately for him, the art critic of the *Morning Post* in 1785, the artist John Hoppner who reviewed the exhibition on May 5, had himself painted individual portraits of the royal princesses for the same exhibition. "So, Mr. Copley, is this the fruit of your long studies and labours? Is it for this you have contemplated the Iris and the Prism? Is it because you have heard *fine feathers* make fine birds, that you have concluded *fine cloaths* will make *Princesses*?

82. *Mrs. John Montresor. 1776.*

What a delightful disorder! Why, you have plucked up harmony by the roots, and planted confusion in its stead! Princesses, parrots, dogs, grapes, flowers, leaves, are each striving for pre-eminence, and opposing, with hostile force, all attempts of our wearied eyes to find repose."

The review was unjustly harsh. Unfortunately its opinions were contagious, and *The Daughters of George III* failed to unleash a flood of commissions from the royal family or the upper nobility. This was unfortunate, because Copley's stylistic gifts were well suited for decorative portraiture, as is evident in the vibrant portraits of *Mrs. Daniel Denison Rogers* (color plate XV, cat. no. 81), Copley's stepniece, and *Mrs. John Montresor* (no. 82), whose husband, a British army officer, Copley had painted in America several years earlier. Like *The Daughters of George III*, these vital female portraits possess the same spontaneity and freedom found in such oil sketches as Copley's portrait of his sister-in-law, *Sarah Startin* (no. 83).

Mrs. Charles Startin. ca. 1783

After the critical buffets of 1785, Copley was undoubtedly more than ready to withdraw and occupy himself with a monumental history painting, *The Siege of Gibraltar* (The Guildhall Museum, London). It was commissioned by the Corporation of the City of London and was the kind of picture with which he had scored his earlier triumphs. The Siege of Gibraltar by the Spanish and their French allies had begun in July, 1779, with a bombardment and blockade. The Spanish moved against Gibraltar on the morning of September 13, 1782, with a fleet of ten specially built, floating batteries or, literally, floating fortresses. After a heavy artillery exchange that lasted throughout the day, one of the batteries broke into flames, illuminating the harbor and permitting the British gunners to fire with deadly accuracy at their helpless targets. Copley initially intended to restrict himself to depicting the terrible scene of the conflagration of the stricken battering ships, and the distressed and writhing figures in the flames and water. The view of the Rock, where General Eliott, his officers and the British emplacements were located, was to be relegated to the background.

By 1786, Copley had sketched the design on a gigantic canvas, 18 × 25 feet, that had been prepared to receive it. A visitor to his studio reported that "The picture was immense; and it was managed by means of a roller, so that any portion of it, at any time, might be easily seen or executed. The artist himself was raised on a platform."[19]

A writer in the *Morning Post* on October 2, 1786, described Copley in his studio as "literally laying siege to Gibraltar, as he has models not only of the fortress, but of gun boats, ship-tackle, men, and every instrument of destruction arranged before him in all the stages of his progress." At that point, some of the officers who had participated in the event objected that the painting did not adequately honor the garrison which had defeated the attacking force at Gibraltar. Copley agreed to introduce a portrait group of officers in the foreground. He also decided to include the Relief of Gibraltar, the ar-

19. Thomas Frognall Dibdin, *Reminiscences of a Literary Life* (London, 1836), 151.

rival of a relief fleet under Admiral Richard Howe, as a long, low predella below the large picture, flanked by medallion portraits of *Admiral Howe* (no. 85), and his second in command, Admiral Barrington.[20]

By the time Copley traveled to Germany in the autumn of 1787 to obtain portrait sketches of the Hanoverian officers who had commanded regiments of mercenaries under Eliott at Gibraltar, such as *Colonels Hugo and Schlepegrell* (no. 86), he must have had the composition of the officer group virtually complete. When all of the portraits had been secured, Copley was able to combine the original sea piece with the completed officers in an oil sketch (no. 84). A dominant element in the picture was to be a sinking Spanish long-

20. Copley actually never painted the Relief of Gibraltar, but subcontracted the commission to the noted marine painter Dominic Serres.

boat in the foreground, with figures clinging to the mast, to each other, and reaching for help from a nearby English gunboat. In the gunboat some of the English sailors turn their attention to rescue operations, while others encourage or actively assist their comrades in the bow of the floating battery above to pull down the Spanish colors (nos. 87 and 88). In the middle distance is another gunboat, beyond which is the giant hulk of a completely shattered, floating battery, swarming with figures in various stages of distress. Sir Roger Curtis directs rescue operations from his boat in the distance. On the right the officers view the action. For the final painting Copley revised the scene in the harbor to integrate it better with the officer group and to bring forward Sir Roger Curtis' longboat (no. 89).

85. Richard, Earl Howe. Befor.

By the spring of 1791, the mammoth *Gibraltar* was finally completed and, despite a tepid critical reception, about sixty thousand people went to see it on exhibition in a magnificent oriental tent in Green Park. In 1793 Copley submitted his first picture in seven years to the annual exhibition of the Royal Academy, *The Red Cross Knight*, (nos. 90 and 91). Depicting a scene from Spenser's *Faerie Queene*, the painting is in fact a group portrait of the now-grown Copley children (John on the left, Elizabeth in the center, Mary on the right). An oval portrait of *John Quincy Adams* (no. 92) also dates from the mid-1790's, a period when portrait commissions were few.

Colonels Hugo and Schlepegrell. 1787

113

D. 1797-'78

87. *Study for* The Siege of Gibraltar. *1785–*

Study for The Siege of Gibraltar. 1785–1786

Study for The Siege of Gibraltar. 1788–1789

91. Sketch for The Red Cross Knight. 1792–

The Red Cross Knight. 1793

92. John Quincy Adams. ca. 1

Sketch for Charles I Demanding in the House of Commons the Five Impeached Members. 1782–1794.

119

94. *Sketch for Monmouth before James II Refusing to Give the Names of Accomplices. 1782–1794*

Study for Monmouth before James II Refusing to Give the Names of His
Accomplices. 1782–1794

In 1795 Copley exhibited his history painting of *King Charles I Demanding in the House of Commons the Five Impeached Members*. He had begun work on the picture fourteen years earlier, after completion of *The Death of Chatham*. This subject, set in the House of Commons, was to be a companion piece to *The Death of Chatham*, which had occurred in the House of Lords. Charles I had gone to the House of Commons on January 4, 1641/2, and demanded the persons of five members accused of treason. His demand, and Speaker Lenthall's memorable response, "I have, Sir, neither eyes to see, nor tongue to speak, in this place, but as the house is pleased to direct me," epitomized the confrontation between the King and Parliament that led to the Civil War.

Copley had to set *Charles I* aside for *The Death of Major Peirson*, but took it up again briefly in 1785 after *The Daughters of George III* was completed. The oil sketch for *Charles I* (no. 93) probably represents the state of the composition late in 1785, when Copley left it again to work on *The Siege of Gibraltar*. He turned back to *Charles I* after *Gibraltar* was finished in 1791, and the picture was finally exhibited publicly on May 5, 1795. This time the public response was clearly unenthusiastic. Copley had attempted to recreate realistically a significant event from the previous century by locating old portraits, grouping them into a cohesive composition and endowing them with appropriate expressions. Although his intention was admirable, he was quite wrong in supposing that his pedantic quest for historical accuracy would interest the public. His achievement was a *tour de force*, but in the end he had expended an enormous amount of time and effort on an artistic dead end. It is probably because he became aware of this that he never finished the large *Monmouth Before James II Refusing to Give the Names of his Accomplices*, which, like *Charles I*, depicted a seventeenth-century event in which a hero refused to betray his fellows to the King. A full oil sketch (no. 94), very similar to the oil sketch for *Charles I*, and a drawing for one of the figures (no. 95), may both date from the early or mid-1780's.

In 1796 Copley exhibited at the Royal Academy *Abraham Offering Up Isaac*; no. 96 is a study for it. It was his first religious subject since *The Tribute Money* of 1782. The following year he painted a splendid life sketch of *Admiral Adam Duncan* (no. 97), shortly after Duncan had become a popular hero by defeating the Dutch in a vicious battle off the coast of Holland at Camperdown. Copley subsequently painted a full-scale history picture of *The Surrender of the Dutch Admiral De Winter to Admiral Duncan, October 11, 1797 (Victory of Duncan)*, depicting the moment when De Winter offered his sword to his conqueror and Duncan, responding gallantly, refused the traditional token of surrender, saying "I would much rather take a brave man's hand than his sword." A drawing for the large painting, squared for transfer, studies a group of background figures on the poop deck raising the flag (no. 98).

On July 3, 1800, Copley's eldest daughter, Elizabeth, married Gardiner Greene, a prosperous Boston widower. Copley began a portrait of her (no. 99), but only the head had been finished by the time she left for Boston. Before Copley could complete the portrait he was forced to set it aside for several important commissions, notably the large *Knatchbull Family*. Not until early in 1803 was he able to complete Elizabeth's portrait, with his other daughter, Mary, modeling the drapery.

Copley was already at work on *The Knatchbull Family* in April, 1801, when Sir Edward Knatchbull, a widower with ten children, married twenty-year-old Mary Hawkins. Sir Edward's new wife had to be included in the composition, and, before long, room had to be made on the canvas for an anticipated infant. The undertaking was further complicated by Sir Edward's wish that his first two wives be shown in some way. Nonetheless Copley completed the picture by the end of 1802. It was unfortunately dismembered sometime during the last century,[21] and an oil sketch for the picture (no. 100), is the primary source of information about it. Copley planned to exhibit

21. It was cut to yield three portraits: a double portrait of Edward and Norton Knatchbull from the left side, young Mary Knatchbull with the tambourine from the center, and Sir Edward Knatchbull, Eighth Bt., from the right side.

96. Study for Abraham Offering Up Isaac. 1795–

Study for The Surrender of the Dutch Admiral De Winter to Admiral Duncan.
1798.

97. Sketch for Adam, Viscount Duncan, Admiral of the White. 1

Mrs. Gardiner Greene. 1800–1803

the large *Knatchbull Family* at the Royal Academy in 1803. However, reports of derision directed at the picture because of the two former wives floating in the upper right among the angels reached Sir Edward and he decided not to allow it to be exhibited. An early drawing (no. 101) shows Norton Knatchbull dressed in a scholar's robes.

The portrait of *Baron Graham* (no. 102), one of four portraits Copley exhibited at the Royal Academy in 1804, is reminiscent of his *Lord Mansfield* (no. 76). In the same year Copley began a large equestrian portrait of the *Prince of Wales* (color plate XVI, cat. no. 103). He hoped to complete it in time for the following year's exhibition, but the project was prolonged by an expansion of the portrait to include attending officers and an encampment in the distance, and by the difficulty involved in persuading the Prince to sit. It was not finished until the middle of 1809, but was prominently displayed at the Royal Academy the following year.

100. Sketch for The Knatchbull Family. 1800–

Copley, now seventy-two years old, hoped that the portrait would win public and critical applause. His reputation had slipped considerably in recent years, especially after his difficulties with the Knatchbull picture in 1803. Instead of achieving security, tranquillity, and honor in the last years of his career, Copley encountered strife, rebuffs, and constant financial worries. Mrs. Copley confided to her daughter in Boston on February 20, 1807, that "your father often regrets that he did not [return to America] many years since,

102. *Sir Robert Graham.*

but these retrospects are vain.''[22] Sadly, but not unexpectedly, Copley's hopes for an artistic comeback with the large equestrian portrait were quickly snuffed out. One reviewer wrote, "A very large canvas, covered with what is not very likely to mislead the public taste. The officers in the back-ground are too diminutive, and make the Prince look like a Brobdignag general at a Lilliputian review. The colouring offends, from the large daubs of deep blue, plastered on in profusion, and relieved by the black hide of the charger that carries his Royal Highness; between whose legs, and in the distance, are seen a host of little figures, seemingly cut out of pasteboard or tin.''[23] Copley's artistic powers had unquestionably declined, but he nevertheless still retained some of his earlier skill. The color is bold, and the portraits on the right are quite effective.

The young American artist, Samuel F. B. Morse, wrote to friends on September 17, 1811: "I visited Mr. Copley a few days since. He is very old and infirm. I think his age is upward of seventy, nearly the age of Mr. West. His powers of mind have almost entirely left him; his late paintings are miserable; it is really a lamentable thing that a man should outlive his faculties. He has been a first-rate painter, as you well know. I saw at his room some exquisite pieces which he painted twenty or thirty years ago, but his paintings of the last four or five years are very bad.[24]

In his old age Copley continued to paint, but the pictures he produced testify to his artistic disintegration during the final few years. He was felled with a stroke in August, 1815, and died peacefully one hundred and fifty years ago, on September 9, 1815, at the age of seventy-seven. After twenty-one years of creative productivity in colonial America and forty more in England, Copley's brush was stilled.

JULES DAVID PROWN
Yale University
New Haven, Connecticut

March 31, 1965

---

22. Amory, *op. cit.*, 284.
23. "Exhibition of Paintings, Somerset House," *The Repository of Arts, Literature, Commerce, Manufactures, Fashions, and Politics,* III (June, 1810), 366.
24. Edward L. Morse, ed., *Samuel F. B. Morse: His Letters and Journals* (Boston and New York, 1914), I, 47.

Selected Bibliography

AMORY, MARTHA BABCOCK, *The Domestic and Artistic Life of John Singleton Copley, R.A.* Boston, 1882.

BAYLEY, FRANK W., *The Life and Works of John Singleton Copley.* Boston, 1915.

BOLTON, THEODORE, AND BINSSE, HARRY LORIN, "John Singleton Copley," *Antiquarian*, XV (December, 1930), 76–83, 116, 118.

BURROUGHS, ALAN, "Young Copley," *Art in America*, XXXI (Oct., 1943), 161–171.

COMSTOCK, HELEN, "Drawings by John Singleton Copley," *Panorama* (Old Print Shop), II (May, 1947).

—, "Drawings by J. S. Copley in the Karolik Collection," *The Connoisseur*, CIX (June, 1942), 150–153.

An Exhibition of Paintings by John Singleton Copley, Metropolitan Museum of Art, Dec. 22, 1936–Feb. 14, 1937. Text by Harry B. Wehle.

FLEXNER, JAMES THOMAS, *John Singleton Copley.* Boston, 1948.

FOOTE, HENRY WILDER, "When was John Singleton Copley Born?" *New England Quarterly*, X (March, 1937), 111–120.

HOWGEGO, JAMES L., "Copley and the Corporation of London," *The Guildhall Miscellany*, IX (July, 1958), 34–43.

John Singleton Copley, 1738–1815. Loan Exhibition, Boston Museum of Fine Arts, Feb. 1–March 15, 1938.

JONES, GUERNSEY, ed., *Letters & Papers of John Singleton Copley and Henry Pelham.* Vol. LXXI of *The Massachusetts Historical Society Collections.* Boston, 1914.

PARKER, BARBARA NEVILLE, AND WHEELER, ANNE BOLLING, *John Singleton Copley: American Portraits.* Boston, 1938.

PARKER, BARBARA NEVILLE., "Problems of Attribution in Early Portraits by Copley," *Bulletin of the Boston Museum of Fine Arts*, XL (June, 1942), 54–57.

PERKINS, AUGUSTUS THORNDIKE, *A Sketch of the Life and A List of Some of the Works of John Singleton Copley.* Boston, 1873.

—, *Supplementary List of Paintings by John Singleton Copley.* Boston, 1875.

PROWN, JULES DAVID, "An 'Anatomy Book' by John Singleton Copley," *Art Quarterly*, XXVI (Spring, 1963), 31–46.

—, "Copley's 'Victory of Duncan,'" *Art in America*, I (1962), 82–85.

—, A monograph on Copley, to be published in March, 1966.

Catalogue

Measurements: Dimensions are given in inches throughout. Height precedes width unless otherwise indicated. The items marked with a (†) are to be shown only at The Metropolitan Museum of Art and the Museum of Fine Arts, Boston. Those marked with an (*) are to be shown only at the National Gallery of Art, Washington. All works are illustrated in the introductory essay.

1. *Reverend William Welsteed*   1753
   Mezzotint, $13\frac{5}{8} \times 9\frac{11}{16}$.
   Signed lower left: *J. S. Copley pint et fecit.*
   Lent by the Yale University Art Gallery, John Hill Morgan Collection.

2. *The Return of Neptune*   ca. 1754
   Oil on canvas, $27\frac{1}{2} \times 44\frac{1}{2}$.
   Unsigned.
   Lent by The Metropolitan Museum of Art, gift of Mrs. Orme Wilson, in memory of her parents, Mr. and Mrs. J. Nelson Borland.

3. *Book of Anatomical Drawings*   1756
   The sketchbook consists of eight drawings by Copley, six of which are signed, and accompanying texts. Black and red chalk and ink on white paper. All of these pages measure $10\frac{3}{4} \times 17\frac{1}{16}$ except plate I, which measures $10\frac{3}{4} \times 16\frac{3}{4}$.
   Lent by The British Museum.

4. *Mrs. Joseph Mann*   1753
   (Bethia Torrey)
   Oil on canvas, $36 \times 27\frac{1}{4}$.
   Signed lower right: *J S Copley Pinx 1753.*
   Lent by the Museum of Fine Arts, Boston.

5. *Charles Pelham*   ca. 1754
   Oil on canvas, 36×28.
   Unsigned.
   The artist's step-brother.
   Lent by Dr. Charles Pelham Curtis.

6. *Ann Gardiner*   ca. 1756
   (Mrs. Arthur Brown)
   Oil on canvas, 50×40.
   Unsigned.
   Lent by the R. H. Gardiner Family.

7. *Jane Browne*   1756
   (Mrs. Samuel Livermore)
   Oil on canvas, $30\frac{1}{8} \times 25\frac{1}{8}$.
   Signed lower right:
   I. S. Copley. Pinx.1756.
   Lent by the National Gallery of Art, Andrew Mellon Collection.

8. *Reverend Arthur Browne*   1757
   Oil on canvas, $29\frac{1}{2} \times 24\frac{1}{2}$.
   Signed lower left:
   I. S. Copley Pinx 1757.
   Lent by the Heritage Foundation, Deerfield, Massachusetts.

9. *Mary and Elizabeth Royall*   ca. 1758
   (Mrs. George Erving and Mrs. William Sparhawk)
   Oil on canvas, $57\frac{1}{2} \times 48$.
   Unsigned.
   Lent by the Museum of Fine Arts, Boston.

10. *Mrs. Thomas Greene*   ca. 1758
    (Martha Coit)
    Oil on canvas, $50\frac{1}{2} \times 40$.
    Unsigned.
    Lent by Mr. and Mrs. Lawrence A. Fleischman.

11. *Reverend Samuel Fayerweather*
    Oil on copper, $3 \times 2\frac{1}{2}$.   ca. 1758
    Unsigned.
    Lent by the Yale University Art Gallery, Mabel Brady Garvan Collection.

12. *Hugh Hall* 1758
Pastel, 15¾ × 12⅞ (sight).
Signed lower right: *J. S. Copley,/
Pinx. 1758.*
Lent by Mr. Michael C. Janeway.

13. *Thaddeus Burr* 1758–1760
Oil on canvas, 50⅝ × 39⅞.
Unsigned.
Lent by the City Art Museum,
St. Louis.

14. *Epes Sargent* 1759–1761
Oil on canvas, 49⅞ × 40.
Unsigned.
Lent by the National Gallery of Art,
gift of the Avalon Foundation.

15. *John Bours* 1758–1761
Oil on canvas, 50¼ × 40⅛.
Unsigned.
Lent by the Worcester Art Museum.

16. *Mrs. Nathaniel Allen* ca. 1763
(Sarah Sargent)
Oil on canvas, 49½ × 40.
Unsigned.
Lent by The Minneapolis Institute
of Arts.

17. *Mrs. Daniel Sargent* 1763
(Mary Turner)
Oil on canvas, 50 × 40.
Signed lower left: *John Singleton
Copley/pinx 1763.*
Lent by Mrs. Thomas R. Symington
(on indefinite loan to the Corcoran
Gallery of Art).

18. *Mrs. Metcalf Bowler* ca. 1763
(Anne Fairchild)
Oil on canvas, 50 × 40.
Unsigned.
Lent by Miss Alida Livingston.

19. *John Scollay* 1764
Pastel, 21⅞ × 16⅞ (sight).
Signed center right: *JSC (monogram)
1764.*
Lent by Mrs. Edward Whitney
Kimball.

20. *Deborah Scollay* ca. 1762
(Mrs. John Melville)
Watercolor on ivory, 1¼ × 1 (sight).
Unsigned.
Lent by the Worcester Art Museum.

21. *Mrs. John Powell* 1764
(Anna Susan Dummer)
Oil on canvas, 49½ × 39½.
Unsigned.
Lent by Mr. Ellery Sedgwick, Jr.

22. *Colonel Nathaniel Sparhawk* 1764
Oil on canvas, 90 × 57½.
Signed center right: *John S.
Copley/pinx 1764.*
Lent by the Museum of Fine Arts,
Boston.

23. *John Hancock* 1765
Oil on canvas, 49½ × 40½.
Signed lower left: *J. S. Copley/pinx
1765.*
President of the Continental Con-
gress, signer of the Declaration of
Independence, and first Governor of
the Commonwealth of Massachusetts.
Lent by the City of Boston, deposited
at the Museum of Fine Arts, Boston.

24. *Mrs. Theodore Atkinson, Jr.* 1765
(Frances Deering Wentworth)
Oil on canvas, 51 × 40.
Signed lower right: *John S. Copley
Pinx/1765.*
Lent by The New York Public
Library.

25. *Mrs. Samuel Waldo* 1764–1765
(Sarah Erving)
Oil on canvas, 50 × 40.
Unsigned.
Lent by Mr. and Mrs. Charles E.
Cotting.

26. *Henry Pelham* (The Boy with
a Squirrel)* 1765
Oil on canvas, 30¼ × 25.
Unsigned.
The sitter was Copley's younger half-
brother, and also an artist. Copley
sent this painting to the exhibition
of the Society of Artists in London
in the spring of 1766, where it was
highly praised by Benjamin West
and Joshua Reynolds.
Lent anonymously.

27. *Mrs. Woodbury Langdon* 1765–1766
(Sarah Sherburne)

Oil on canvas, 49¾ × 39¾.
Unsigned.
Lent by Mrs. Thomas B. Foster.

28. *Nathaniel Hurd*   ca. 1765
Oil on canvas, 30 × 25½.
The sitter was a Boston silversmith
and engraver.
Lent by The Cleveland Museum of
Art, John Huntington Collection.

29. *Nicholas Boylston*   1767
Oil on canvas, 49 × 40.
Signed lower left: *JSC* (*monogram*)
1767.
Lent by Harvard University.

30. *Mrs. Thomas Boylston*   1766
(Sarah Morecock)
Oil on canvas, 50½ × 40¼.
Signed center right: *Jnᵒ S.*
Copley/pinx 1766.
Lent by Harvard University.

31. *Judge Martin Howard*   1767
Oil on canvas, 49½ × 39¾.
Signed center right: *JSC* (*monogram*)
1767.
Lent by the Proprietors of the Social
Law Library, Boston.

32. *Mrs. Joseph Greene*   1767
(Mary Greene)
Pastel, 23¼ × 17¼.
Signed lower right: *J. S.*
Copley./pinx 1767.
Lent by Mrs. Allan Forbes.

33. *Mrs. Joseph Barrell*   ca. 1771
(Hannah Fitch)
Pastel, 23 × 17¼.
Unsigned.
Lent by the Museum of Fine Arts,
Boston.

34. *Jonathan Jackson*   1767–1769
Pastel, 23 × 17 (sight).
Unsigned.
Lent by Mr. Francis W. Peabody.

35. *Governor John Wentworth*   1769
Pastel, 23 × 17½ (sight).
Signed center right: *JSC* (*mono-
gram*) *p.1769.*

Royal Governor of New Hampshire
from 1766 to 1775.
Lent by Mr. and Mrs. Gordon
Abbott.

36. *Samuel Cary*   ca. 1769
Watercolor on ivory, 1⁷⁄₁₆ × 1³⁄₁₆.
Unsigned.
Lent by Mr. and Mrs. Edward
Cunningham.

37. *Mrs. Samuel Cary*   ca. 1769
(Sarah Gray)
Watercolor on ivory, 1³⁄₈ × 1³⁄₁₆.
Signed lower right: *JSC* (*monogram*).
Lent by Mr. and Mrs. Edward
Cunningham.

38. *Mrs. Jerathmael Bowers*   1767–1770
(Mary Sherburne)
Oil on canvas, 49¾ × 39¾.
Unsigned.
Lent by The Metropolitan Museum
of Art, Rogers Fund.

39. *Isaac Smith*   1769
Oil on canvas, 49¼ × 39½.
Unsigned.
Lent by the Yale University Art
Gallery, Maitland F. Griggs
Collection.

40. *Mrs. Isaac Smith*   1769
(Elizabeth Storer)
Oil on canvas, 50⅛ × 40⅛.
Unsigned.
Lent by the Yale University Art
Gallery, Maitland F. Griggs
Collection.

41. *Jeremiah Lee*   1769
Oil on canvas, 94⅞ × 58⅞.
Signed center left: *JSC* (*monogram*)
P.1769.
Lent by the Wadsworth Atheneum,
Hartford, The Ella Gallup Sumner
and Mary Catlin Sumner Collection.

42. *Mrs. Jeremiah Lee*   1769
(Martha Swett)
Oil on canvas, 94⅞ × 58⅞.
Signed lower left: *JSC* (*monogram*)
P.1769.
Lent by the Wadsworth Atheneum,

Hartford, The Ella Gallup Sumner
and Mary Catlin Sumner Collection.

43. *Mrs. Ezekiel Goldthwait*   1770–1771
(Elizabeth Lewis)
Oil on canvas, 50 × 39¾.
Unsigned.
Lent by the Museum of Fine Arts,
Boston.

44. *Mrs. Samuel Watts*   ca. 1770
(Sarah Osborne)
Oil on canvas, 29 × 24.
Unsigned.
Lent by Mr. Frederick S. Moseley, Jr.

45. *Paul Revere*   1768–1770
Oil on canvas, 35 × 28½.
Unsigned.
Lent by the Museum of Fine Arts,
Boston.

46. *Mrs. Humphrey Devereux*   1771
(Mary Charnock)
Oil on canvas, 40⅛ × 32.
Signed lower right: *C . . . 1771.*
The sitter was the mother of John
Greenwood, the Boston portrait
painter. Lent by the National Art
Gallery, New Zealand, and the
Greenwood Family.

47. *General Thomas Gage*   1768–1769
Oil on canvas, 50 × 39¾.
Unsigned.
Commander of British troops in
Boston in 1775. He ordered the arrest
of Samuel Adams and John Hancock
and sent the colonial militia to
Lexington and Concord, which led
to the first bloodshed of the
Revolution.
Lent by Mrs. Harriet Moseley
Bodley.

48. *Samuel Adams*   1770–1772
Oil on canvas, 50 × 40¼.
Unsigned.
The sitter was a radical Whig
leader and later three times
Governor of the Commonwealth of
Massachusetts.
Lent by the City of Boston, deposited
at the Museum of Fine Arts, Boston.

49. *Thomas Flucker*   1770–1772
Oil on canvas, 28 × 23.
Unsigned.
Lent by the Bowdoin College
Museum of Art.

50. *Mrs. Richard Skinner*   1772
(Dorothy Wendell)
Oil on canvas, 39¾ × 30¾.
Signed center right: *John Singleton
Copley. pinx/1772/Boston.*
Lent by the Museum of Fine Arts,
Boston.

51. *Mrs. Moses Gill*   ca. 1773
(Rebecca Boylston)
Oil on canvas, 49¾ × 39½.
Unsigned.
Lent by the Museum of Art, Rhode
Island School of Design.

52. *Reverend Thomas Cary*   1773
Oil on canvas, 50 × 40¼.
Unsigned.
Lent by the Museum of Fine Arts,
Boston.

53. *Eleazer Tyng*   1772
Oil on canvas, 49⅞ × 40⅛.
Signed lower left: *John Singleton
Copley/pinx 1772. Boston.*
Lent by the National Gallery of Art,
gift of the Avalon Foundation.

54. *John Winthrop*   ca. 1773
Oil on canvas, 50¼ × 40¼.
Unsigned.
Professor at Harvard and America's
first prominent astronomer.
Lent by Harvard University.

55. *Mr. and Mrs. Thomas Mifflin*   1773
(Sarah Morris)
Oil on canvas, 60½ × 48.
Signed upper right: *J. Singleton
Copley.Pinx./1773. Boston.*
Thomas Mifflin was later aide-de-
camp to General Washington, a
Major-General and Quartermaster
General of the Revolutionary Army,
and Governor of Pennsylvania.
Lent by The Historical Society of
Pennsylvania.

56. *Mr. and Mrs. Isaac Winslow*   1774
(Jemima Debuke)
Oil on canvas, 40¼ × 48¾.
Unsigned.
Lent by the Museum of Fine Arts,
Boston.

57. *Roman Conquest*   1774–1775
Black and white chalk on blue-gray
paper, 13½ × 30.
Unsigned.
Lent by the Addison Gallery of
American Art, Phillips Academy,
Andover, Massachusetts.

58. *The Ascension*   1775
Oil on canvas, 32 × 29.
Unsigned.
Painted in Rome.
Lent by the Museum of Fine Arts,
Boston.

59. Study for *The Ascension*   1774–1775
Sepia wash and pencil on buff paper,
15⅛ × 20½.
Unsigned.
See no. 58.
Lent by The Metropolitan Museum
of Art, Dick Fund.

60. *Mr. and Mrs. Ralph Izard*   1775
(Alice Delancey)
Oil on canvas, 69 × 88½.
Unsigned.
Painted in Rome.
Lent by the Museum of Fine Arts,
Boston.

61. *The Copley Family*   1776–1777
Oil on canvas, 72½ × 90⅜.
Unsigned.
The artist appears at the upper left.
Below him sits his father-in-law,
Richard Clarke, agent of the East
India Company and one of the
consignees of the cargo of tea thrown
into the harbor at the Boston Tea
Party. Clarke holds on his lap
Copley's youngest child, Susanna.
Next to him stands Elizabeth, and to
the right are John Singleton Copley,
Jr., Mrs. Copley, and Mary.
Lent by the National Gallery of Art,
Washington, Andrew Mellon Fund.

62. Sketch for *The Copley Family*   1776
Oil on canvas, 20¾ × 26½.
Unsigned.
See no. 61.
Lent anonymously.

63. Study for *The Nativity*   1776
Black, white and red chalk on blue-
gray grounded white paper,
10⅝ × 15⅜.
Unsigned.
Lent by Mr. and Mrs. Jules David
Prown.

64. *Self-Portrait*   1776–1780
Oil on canvas, 18⅛ diameter.
Unsigned.
Lent anonymously.

65. *Squire Robert Hyde of Hyde*   1778
Oil on canvas, 29¾ × 24¾.
Signed lower left: *J. S. Copley
Pinx/1778.*
Lent by The Art Institute of Chicago,
Friends of American Art Collection.

66. *Sir William Pepperrell
and His Family*   1778
Oil on canvas, 90 × 108.
Signed lower left: *J. S. Copley
P.1778.*
Lent by the North Carolina Museum
of Art, Raleigh.

67. Study for *Sir William*   1777–1778
Pepperrell and His Family
Black and white chalk on buff paper,
17¾ × 10⅞.
Unsigned.
See no. 66.
Lent by The Victoria and Albert
Museum, London.

68a. *Watson and the Shark**   1778
Oil on canvas, 71¾ × 90½.
Signed center left: *J S Copley.
P. 1778–*
Young Brook Watson was attacked
by a shark while swimming in Havana
Harbor. He lost a leg before being
rescued.
Lent by the National Gallery of Art,
Ferdinand Lammot Belin Fund.

68b. *Watson and the Shark*† 1778
Oil on canvas, 72⅛ × 90¼.
Signed center left: *J. S. Copley.
P.1778.*
Another version of 68a.
Lent by the Museum of Fine Arts,
Boston.

69. *Head of a Negro* 1777–1783
Oil on canvas, 21 × 16¼.
Unsigned.
Quite possibly the same subject who
appears in *Watson and the Shark.*
Lent by The Detroit Institute of Arts.

70. *The Death of the Earl of Chatham*
1779–1781
Oil on canvas, 90 × 121.
Unsigned.
The elder Pitt, the Earl of Chatham,
while addressing the House of Lords,
suffered a stroke from which he
never recovered.
Lent by the Trustees of the Tate
Gallery, London.

71. Sketch for *The Death of the Earl of
Chatham* 1779
Oil on canvas, 20¾ × 25⅜.
Signed lower right: *J S Copley/1779.*
See no. 70.
Lent by the National Gallery of Art,
gift of Mrs. Gordon Dexter.

72. Study of Richard Brock-
lesby for *The Death of the
Earl of Chatham* 1779–1780
Black and white chalk on gray paper,
27½ × 21½.
Unsigned.
See no. 70.
Lent by the Boston Athenaeum.

73. *Elkanah Watson* 1782
Oil on canvas, 58⅝ × 47⅝.
Unsigned.
Lent by The Art Museum, Princeton
University, Estate of Josephine
Thomson Swann.

74. *The Tribute Money* 1782
Oil on canvas, 50½ × 60½.
Unsigned.

Copley's "diploma" picture for the
Royal Academy.
Lent by The Royal Academy of Arts,
London.

75. *Midshipman Augustus Brine* 1782
Oil on canvas, 49½ × 39½.
Signed: *J.S. Copley Pin . . . /1782.*
Lent by The Metropolitan Museum
of Art, bequest of Richard deWolfe
Brixey.

76. *William Murray, First Earl
of Mansfield* 1783
Oil on canvas, 88 × 57½.
Signed lower right: *J. S. Copley, pinx.*
Lent by the National Portrait
Gallery, London.

77. *The Death of Major Peirson* 1782–1784
Oil on canvas, 97 × 144.
Unsigned.
In 1781, Major Peirson, refusing to
accept surrender, rallied dispersed
English troops and repulsed the in-
vading French forces which had all
but won the Isle of Jersey. At the
moment of victory, the young officer
was mortally wounded.
Lent by the Trustees of the Tate
Gallery, London.

78. Study for *The Death of Major Peirson*
1782–1783
Black and white chalk on gray-blue
paper, 13⅞ × 22¼.
Unsigned.
See no. 77.
Lent by the Museum of Fine Arts,
Boston.

79. Study for *The Death of Major Peirson*
1782–1783
Black and white chalk on gray-blue
paper, 13⅝ × 22⅜.
Unsigned.
See no. 77.
Lent by the Museum of Fine Arts,
Boston.

80. *The Three Princesses* 1785
(The daughters of George III)
Oil on canvas, 104½ × 73.

Signed lower left: *J. S. Copley R.A. 1785.*
(Photo: A. C. Cooper [Colour] Limited: Copyright Reserved).
Lent by H. M. Queen Elizabeth II.

81. *Mrs. Daniel Denison Rogers* (Abigail Bromfield)   1783–1788
Oil on canvas, 50 × 40.
Unsigned.
Lent anonymously.

82. *Mrs. John Montresor*   1776–1780
(Frances Tucker)
Oil on canvas, 30⅜ × 25⅛.
Signed center right: *J S Copley. .7 . .*
Lent by Mr. and Mrs. Richard I. Robinson.

83. *Mrs. Charles Startin*   ca. 1783
(Sarah Clarke)
Oil on canvas, 23¾ × 19¾.
Unsigned.
The artist's sister-in-law.
Lent by Mr. and Mrs. William P. Wadsworth.

84. Sketch for *The Siege of Gibraltar* 1788
Oil on canvas, 36 × 50½.
Unsigned.
The scene depicts the defeat of the Spanish floating batteries by the British garrison at Gibraltar, September 13, 1782.
Lent by the Thomas Coram Foundation for Children.

85. *Richard, Earl Howe*   before 1794
Oil on canvas. 30 × 30 (painted circle).
Unsigned.
Admiral of the Fleet and British Commander-in-Chief in North America during the Revolution, 1776–1778.
Lent by the Trustees of the National Maritime Museum, London.

86. *Colonels Hugo and Schlepegrell*   1787
(Sketch for *The Siege of Gibraltar*)
Oil on canvas, 26 × 22.
Unsigned.
German officers who commanded mercenary regiments during the siege of Gibraltar.

See no. 84.
Lent by the Fogg Art Musem, Harvard University, gift of Mrs. Gordon Dexter.

87. Study for *The Siege of Gibraltar* 1785–1786
Black and white chalk on gray-blue paper, 14 × 8¹¹⁄₁₆.
Unsigned.
See no. 84.
Lent by The Victoria and Albert Museum, London.

88. Study for *The Siege of Gibraltar* 1785–1786
Black and white chalk on blue paper, 13¾ × 20¾.
Unsigned.
See no. 84.
Lent by the Museum of Fine Arts, Boston.

89. Study for *The Siege of Gibraltar* 1788–1789
Black, white and red chalk on gray-blue paper, 19¾ × 37.
Unsigned.
See no. 84.
Lent by The Victoria and Albert Museum, London.

90. *The Red Cross Knight*   1793
Oil on canvas, 84 × 107½.
Unsigned.
The allegorical subject is taken from Edmund Spenser's *Faerie Queene*, Book I, Canto X. The figures, assuming the roles of the Red Cross Knight, Faith, and Hope, are the artist's children, John, Elizabeth, and Mary.
Lent by the National Gallery of Art, gift of Mrs. Gordon Dexter.

91. Sketch for *The Red Cross Knight* 1792–1793
Oil on canvas, 17 × 21.
Unsigned.
See no. 90.
Lent by Mr. and Mrs. Paul Mellon.

92. *John Quincy Adams*   ca. 1796
Oil on canvas, 30 × 25.
Unsigned.

Lent by the Museum of Fine Arts, Boston.

93. Sketch for *Charles I Demanding in the House of Commons the Five Impeached Members*   1782–1794
Oil on canvas, 24¼ × 29.
Unsigned.
Charles, in his struggle with the House of Commons, demanded the surrender of five members on the grounds of high treason with the Scots. The House, asserting its own rights, refused to comply.
Lent by the Fogg Art Museum, Harvard University, gift of Mr. Copley Amory, Jr.

94. Sketch for *Monmouth before James II Refusing to Give the Names of His Accomplices*   1782–1794
Oil on canvas, 24¾ × 29⅝.
Unsigned.
Lent by the Fogg Art Museum, Harvard University, gift of Mr. Copley Amory, Jr.

95. Study for *Monmouth before James II Refusing to Give the Names of His Accomplices*   1782–1794
Pencil and white chalk on blue paper, 13¾ × 11¼.
Signed lower left: *J. S. Copley*.
See no. 94.
Lent by the Fogg Art Museum, Harvard University, Louis E. Bettens Fund.

96. Study for *Abraham Offering Up Isaac*   1795–1796
Black chalk on white paper, 16⅜ × 12½.
Unsigned.
Lent by the Addison Gallery of American Art, Phillips Academy, Andover, Massachusetts.

97. Sketch for *Adam, Viscount Duncan, Admiral of the White*   1797
Oil on canvas, 22½ × 19⅜.
Unsigned.
Admiral Duncan commanded a British blockade that trapped the Dutch fleet off the coast of Holland near Camperdown in the fall of 1797, and decisively defeated it in a bloody battle.
Lent by the Yale University Art Gallery.

98. Study for *The Surrender of the Dutch Admiral De Winter to Admiral Duncan*   1798
Black, white and red chalk on gray-blue paper, 12⅜ × 9.
Unsigned.
Lent by The Metropolitan Museum of Art, Dick Fund.

99. *Mrs. Gardiner Greene*   1800–1803
(Elizabeth Copley)
Oil on canvas, 30¾ × 25¾.
Unsigned.
The artist's eldest child.
Lent by Mrs. Copley Amory.

100. Sketch for *The Knatchbull Family*   1800–1802
Oil on canvas, 25½ × 37½.
Unsigned.
Lent by The Lord Brabourne.

101. Study for *The Knatchbull Family*   1800–1802
Pencil and white chalk on blue-gray paper, 13⅜ × 11.
Unsigned.
Edward Knatchbull, later 9th Baronet, and Norton Knatchbull.
See no. 100.
Lent by the F. M. Hall Collection, University of Nebraska Art Galleries.

102. *Sir Robert Graham*   1804
Oil on canvas, 57¼ × 46⅞.
Signed left center: *J S Copley R.A. pinx*.
Shown as a baron of the Exchequer.
Lent by the National Gallery of Art, Washington, gift of Mrs. Gordon Dexter.

103. *George IV as Prince of Wales*   1804–1810
Oil on canvas. 147½ × 125½.
Unsigned.
Lent by the Museum of Fine Arts, Boston.

DATE DUE
REMINDER

MAY 1 2 2000

**Please do not remove
this date due slip.**